The United States

New Hampshire

Anne Welsbacher
ABDO & Daughters

visit us at
www.abdopub.com

Published by Abdo & Daughters, 4940 Viking Drive, Suite 622, Edina, Minnesota 55435. Copyright © 1998 by Abdo Consulting Group, Inc., Pentagon Tower, P.O. Box 36036, Minneapolis, Minnesota 55435 USA. International copyrights reserved in all countries. No part of this book may be reproduced in any form without written permission from the publisher.

Printed in the United States.

Cover and Interior Photo credits: Peter Arnold, Inc., SuperStock, Archive

Edited by Lori Kinstad Pupeza
Contributing editor Brooke Henderson
Special thanks to our Checkerboard Kids—Grace Hansen, Tyler Shane, Peter Dumdei

All statistics taken from the 1990 census; The Rand McNally Discovery Atlas of The United States.

Library of Congress Cataloging-in-Publication Data

Welsbacher, Anne, 1955-
    New Hampshire / Anne Welsbacher.
    p. cm. -- (United States)
    Includes index.
    Summary: Surveys the history, geography, and people of the state sometimes called the Primary State.
    ISBN 1-56239-888-1
    1. New Hampshire--Juvenile literature. [1. New Hampshire.]
    I. Title. II. Series: United States (Series)
    F34.3.W45 1998
    974.2--dc21
                                         97-27135
                                         CIP
                                       AC

Contents

Welcome to New Hampshire

New Hampshire is a great state to visit all year long. Many lakes and beaches make summertime fun. In the fall lots of New Hampshire's trees turn pretty colors. Wintertime visitors can ski down its mountains.

New Hampshire was the first state to break away from England. New Hampshire's vote passed the most important law in the United States: the **Constitution**. The first **primary election** is held in New Hampshire each time we elect a president.

There is a kind of rock in much of New Hampshire's land. It is called granite. For this reason, New Hampshire is called the Granite State.

A New Hampshire forest during fall.

Fast Facts

NEW HAMPSHIRE

Capital
Concord (36,006 people)
Area
8,992 square miles
(23,289 sq km)
Population
1,113,915 people
Rank: 41st
Statehood
June 21, 1788
(9th state admitted)
Principal rivers
Connecticut River
Merrimack River
Highest point
Mount Washington;
6,288 feet (1,917 m)
Largest city
Manchester (99,567 people)
Motto
Live free or die
Song
"Old New Hampshire"
Famous People
Mary Baker Eddy, Robert Frost,
Horace Greeley, Franklin Pierce,
Alan B. Shepard

New Hampshire is one of the original 13 colonies

13

*P*urple Lilac

*S*tate Flag

*P*urple Finch

*W*hite Birch

About New Hampshire
The Granite State

Detail area

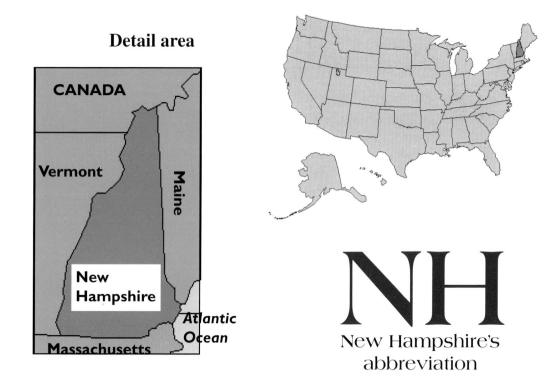

CANADA

Vermont

Maine

New Hampshire

Atlantic Ocean

Massachusetts

NH

New Hampshire's abbreviation

Borders: west (Vermont), north (Canada), east (Maine, Atlantic Ocean), south (Massachusetts)

Nature's Treasures

Trees cover most of New Hampshire. **Lumber** was an important resource in early New Hampshire. Today, the trees also provide maple syrup and sugar.

The land holds granite, sand, and gravel. But because of all the trees, few of these minerals are mined out of the land.

The weather in New Hampshire is cool. Winter can get very cold and snowy. Some mountains in New Hampshire can get 100 inches (254 cm) of snow in a year!

New Hampshire has many rivers and lakes. The rivers supply water power to run things. The largest lake, Lake Winnipesaukee, is 70 square miles (180 sq km) around!

Boathouses on Lake Winnipesaukee, New Hampshire.

Beginnings

About 10,000 years ago, Native Americans first came to New Hampshire. In the 1600s, English people **claimed** New Hampshire as England's third **colony**. In January, 1776, New Hampshire wrote its first **constitution**. New Hampshire was the first colony to write its own constitution.

On July 4, 1776, New Hampshire and the other colonies signed the Declaration of Independence. This said they were a new country. Then they fought and won the **Revolutionary War** against England. They became the United States of America.

In 1788, the United States wrote a new constitution. Each of the 13 colonies could vote for or against the Constitution. If a colony voted for it, it became a state. Nine votes were needed to make the Constitution the new law for the new United States.

New Hampshire was the ninth **colony** to vote yes. So New Hampshire's vote passed the new United States **Constitution**. It also made New Hampshire the ninth state.

New Hampshire was a farming state. But in the 1800s, it also had railroads, ships, and factories. Cotton, shoes, paper, ships, and wagons were some of the things made in New Hampshire.

Each state has a "primary" election to pick who will run for president. In 1909, and from that time on, New Hampshire held the country's first **primary election**. Every election year, people watch to see how New Hampshire will vote. So this is why New Hampshire is called the Primary State.

New Hampshire took part in the Revolutionary War.

1600s to Early 1700s

Early Times

 1600s: Algonquians live in New Hampshire area. English settlers arrive.

 1638: Exeter is **founded** by a minister who came to New Hampshire because he wanted free choice in religion.

 Early 1700s: Irish settlers begin to grow potatoes. Potatoes later become a big crop in the United States.

New Hampshire

1600s to Early 1700s

13

Late 1700s

A New Country

1776: New Hampshire writes its first **constitution**. New Hampshire and other states sign the Declaration of Independence.

1777: The *Ranger* sails. Built in New Hampshire, the *Ranger* is the first war ship to fly the American flag in the **Revolutionary War**.

1788: New Hampshire becomes the ninth state.

New Hampshire

Late 1700s

1800s to 1900s

Into the Future

 1804: The first cotton mill is built in New Ipswich.

 1950s: Computers and televisions are made in New Hampshire.

 1961: Alan B. Shepard, Jr., from New Hampshire, takes the first flight into space.

New Hampshire

1800s to 1900s

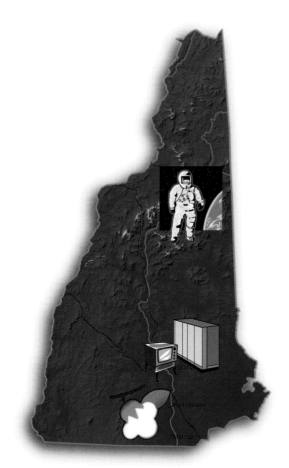

17

New Hampshire's People

There are around 1.1 million people living in New Hampshire. About half live in cities. The other half live in **rural** areas.

Siblings Barbara Ann, Robert, and Linda Cochran were born in New Hampshire. Along with their sister Marilyn, the Cochrans won honors as skiers. Barbara won a gold medal at the Olympics in 1972.

The newspaper editor Horace Greeley was from Amherst, New Hampshire. The leader and speechmaker Daniel Webster was born in Salisbury. And the writer John Irving is from Exeter.

The astronaut Alan B. Shepard, Jr., was born in New Hampshire. Sarah Josepha Hale, who wrote the song "Mary Had a Little Lamb," was from Newport. And Laura Bridgman, the first deaf and blind person to learn reading and writing, was from Hanover.

Supreme Court judges Salmon Portland Chase and Harlan Fiske Stone were from New Hampshire. Passaconaway, a Pennacook chief who lived in the 1500s and 1600s, was from the area now called New Hampshire. He was about 100 years old when he died!

Sharon Christa McAuliffe lived in Concord. She taught social studies at a school there. She was chosen to be part of the crew on the space shuttle Challenger. Tragically, on January 28, 1986, the space shuttle exploded just moments after take off.

Sharon Christa McAuliffe

John Irving

Alan B. Shepard, Jr.

New Hampshire's Cities

Manchester is the largest city in New Hampshire. Nashua is the next largest. Concord is the capital of New Hampshire and its third largest city. All three cities are in the south-central part of the state.

Rochester is the next largest city. It is in the southeast part of the state, along the **border** of Maine.

Portsmouth is the next largest city. **Port** means a "gate" that opens up to the sea. The end of a river is sometimes called its **mouth**. Can you guess where Portsmouth might be? If you guessed next to the sea and at the mouth of a river, you guessed right!

Concord

Rochester

Manchester

Nashua

Portsmouth

20

The New Hampshire State Capitol.

New Hampshire's Land

New Hampshire is shaped like a saw standing on its handle. The blade is the long western **border** of the state. The dull side is the straight eastern border. The tip pokes up to Canada!

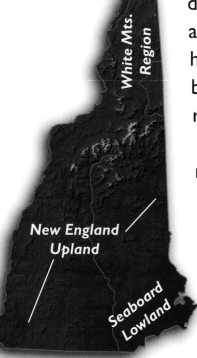

White Mts. Region

New England Upland

Seaboard Lowland

New Hampshire's land has three different regions. The Seaboard Lowlands are in the southeastern corner—near the handle of the saw. Here there are beaches on the Atlantic Ocean and many rivers.

The New England Upland is the biggest region. It covers the middle part of the state. It has valleys, hills, rivers, and lakes. The Merrimack River runs through the middle of this region.

The White Mountains cover the northern third of the state. The area is covered with rugged mountains and deep valleys. Mount Washington, in the Presidential Range of the White Mountains, is the highest point in the state. Mount Washington towers over all the other mountains in the east. From its peak people can see three other states, Canada, and the Atlantic Ocean!

Throughout the state, New Hampshire's forests are filled with ash, beech, birch, cedar, elm, fir, oak, and pine trees.

Mount Washington in the White Mountains National Forest, New Hampshire.

New Hampshire at Play

New Hampshire is famous for its winter sports! People come from everywhere to ski the snow-topped mountains. After skiing, they can warm up next to the fire at one of New Hampshire's lodges.

New Hampshirites celebrate many winter carnivals throughout the state. The carnivals have skiing, skating, hockey, and ice sculpture contests. There is even a sled dog race!

The White Mountains are fun in the summer, too. People hike, camp, and mountain climb. At the lakes, people water ski, swim, and canoe.

Many writers and artists have worked in New Hampshire. The play *Our Town,* by Thorton Wilder, is about a make-believe New Hampshire town. It was written while Wilder lived in New Hampshire. Poet

Robert Frost and J.D. Salinger also wrote while in New Hampshire.

The Sheep and Wool Festival takes place every May in New Boston. In the fall, people can visit the Riverfest Celebration, the Sandwich Fair, or the Candlelight Stroll. New Hampshire also has horse shows and motorcycle races.

Skiing is popular in New Hampshire.

New Hampshire at Work

Many New Hampshirites work in **manufacturing**. They make computers, televisions, car parts, radios, and shoes. Many sell these products.

New Hampshirites work as nurses, bankers, or car repair people. They also work in hotels, motels, cafes, and lodges.

A few people farm. They keep cows for milk. They gather maple syrup from the trees. They also grow apples and potatoes.

Some people fish. They catch lobsters, clams, and cod. Others mine gravel from the land. After all, New Hampshire is the Granite State!

Cows grazing in a field in New Hampshire.

Fun Facts

- The first public library in the United States opened in Peterborough, New Hampshire, in 1833.
- The oldest pipe organ in the United States is the Brattle organ in Portsmouth, in St. John's Episcopal Church. It was built in England around 1708. The organ is still played for special events.
- The shortest ocean coast in the United States is in New Hampshire. It is 18 miles (29 km) long.
- Two New Hampshire towns are named Rye and Sandwich.
- The first college boat race was held in 1852. It was between Harvard and Yale on Lake Winnipesaukee.
- The first library law was made in New Hampshire in 1849. The law let cities use tax money to help build libraries.

•The Craftsmen's Fair, held every summer in Mount Sunapee, is the oldest crafts fair in the United States. The fair, which lasts nine days, has been held since the early 1930s.

•There is a group of rocks on the White Mountains in New Hampshire that looks like a man's face from the side. It has been named the Old Man of the Mountain.

Old Man of the Mountain.

Glossary

Border: the edge of something.

Claim: to take.

Colony: a place owned by another country.

Constitution: a set of laws written by the people, not a king.

Founded: to start or set up something new.

Lumber: wood that has been cut so it can be used to build things.

Manufacture: to make things.

Mouth: used to describe the end of a river.

Port: a "gate" that opens up to the sea.

Primary election: an early election held to help United States citizens pick the people who they want to run for president.

Revolutionary War: The war in which America won its independence from Great Britain. Also called the American Revolution.

Rural: in the country, not the city.

Sibling: a brother or a sister.

Internet Sites

The New Hampshire Almanac
http://www.state.nh.us/nhinfo/nhinfo.html
The State of New Hampshire has produced a number of resources and publications on the Internet that include New Hampshire history, state government, famous people, New Hampshire's firsts, cities and towns, state icons and trivia, and much much more.

NH.com
http://www.nh.com/
This site includes a Governor's page, a what's new section, weather watch, and a New Hampshire directory. Also included are education, environment, facts & fun, history, and more.

These sites are subject to change. Go to your favorite search engine and type in New Hampshire for more sites.

PASS IT ON

Tell Others Something Special About Your State

To educate readers around the country, pass on interesting tips, places to see, history, and little unknown facts about the state you live in. We want to hear from you!

To get posted on ABDO & Daughters website, E-mail us at "mystate@abdopub.com"

Index